A Natural History of the Tribes of Mutant Thoughts

A Natural History of the Tribes of Mutant Thoughts

Poems and Doggerel

Gordon Davis

Essex Editions

Copyright © 2018 by Gordon Davis
Cover art by Melissa Davis
Cover design by George Davis

All rights reserved. No part of this book may be reproduced or transmitted in any form or by any means, electronic or mechanical, including photocopying, recording or by any information storage and retrieval system, without written permission from the publisher, except for the inclusion of brief quotations in a review.

Published in the United States by Essex Editions.

ISBN-10: 0-9967870-8-9
ISBN-13: 978-0-9967870-8-6
Library of Congress Control Number: 2018967136

Essex Editions
Post Office Box 25
Essex, New York 12936
www.essexeditions.com
contact@essexeditions.com

To the poets who'd rather write verses than read those penned by others, yet who compliment me by their reading of these lines.

TABLE OF CONTENTS

POET'S CHALLENGE 1
SPECTERS ON THE SHORE 3
DISPUTES 4
EQUINOX 5
FELLOW TRAVELERS 6
HANGZHOU 9
THE CONNOISSEUR OF CHEEKBONES 10
ECHOES 12
FATHER 13
SHUCKING THE BAPTIST BACKPACK 14
CASTING THE RUNES 16
TOUR GUIDE 17
CHRISTIANS AND LIONS 19
FATHER AT THE MARGIN 20
BEACHES 22
VIXEN 25
BERNICE 26
TIRE IRON 29
DEATH AND TAXES 32
MANAGER'S CALL 35
LATE IN THE DAY 37
SELF HELP 39
LEFT HANGING 40

OUT BACK	41
MEN'S EUROPEAN FIGURE SKATING CHAMPIONSHIPS 1994	42
WHERE HAVE YOU GONE, JOE DIMAGGIO?	43
THE ACTOR	46
NAMES	47
THIRTIETH COLLEGE REUNION	49
FIFTIETH HIGH SCHOOL REUNION	52
HOLY LAND UPDATE	55
GOP EMPATHY, TO BE CONTINUED	56
TO MY CHINESE COLLEAGUES	57
SMOKING IN A BEIJING TAXI	58
MOTHER'S FUNERAL	61
MABEL AND MARGARET	64
THE PRIZED IF UNFORESEEN REWARD	67
ANCIENT AND ABRADED HILLS	68
SIXTY	69
THE ANARCHY OF A ONCE WELL-DISCIPLINED ANATOMY	71
UNWELCOME AUTUMN	72
DARKNESS	74
POSTSCRIPT	76

POET'S CHALLENGE

The challenge for the poet, or his fate,
Is to surrender to the undertow that
Draws him into deeper water
Where the formidable breaker
First auditions as a modest swell.

If at first unprepossessing,
It gathers strength and then, progressing
Lifts him up and lets him down
As, smitten by the nearness of the beach
It flexes, summons its reserves,
Gathers speed and energy,
And plunges dissolutely toward the sand.

It will have moved him only slightly
As it passes,
But he'll have recognized its portent
And foreseen its rush
To dank perdition
Heralded by plumes of sputum
Spinning off its crest
As it collapses on the waiting shingle
That remains unmoved and unimpressed.
He will have heard the anguished roar as it
      expires,
Prostrated on the beach of dashed desires.

Now swim in through the foam and splatter
And immortalize the moment.
Scratch the record in the sand,
This exercise is for the poet's benefit alone,
And if it quickly disappears unread, no matter.

The poet pens a natural history of the
Tribes of mutant thoughts that, seriatim,
Occupy and then, in turn, succumb, but leave no
Fossil record of their fleeting domination
Other than his imprecise transcription
Written for himself alone,
This terra is cognita to him only,
And is its own reward.

SPECTERS ON THE SHORE

Late morning and with nothing left to read,
Attention strays to lowering clouds
And drifting mist along the shore,
Its strands and tendrils braiding into dervishes

That swirl portentously
But lack a pattern or design
Until a rising offshore breeze
Persuades these brooding mystics to disperse

Revealing self-important herring gulls
That stride along the shore.
Could be a promenade of cassocked priests
Attended by a retinue

Of sandpipers like altar boys.
Mincing, chins tucked in,
As unmistakable as if
They brandished censers

And a brazen cross.
But to what end?
A paradigm of holiness?
Or nothing more than specters on the shore?

DISPUTES

Disputes logged to memory
Turn trivial in retrospect,
Neither raptures nor nightmares.
Silly litigations on behalf of clients now forgotten,
Controversies over noise in an apartment,
Banalities of a prior marriage,
Bickering directors on a bank board,
Confronting mental illness in a colleague,
Hardly worth the time it took to tell, much less to
      live.

And yet these tempests raged
And occupied all psychic space,
They surged and blew
And blocked the sun at noon.
They brought one to one's knees.
One somehow felt one's way,
Traversed those minefields, slogged through
The sucking mud,
Everything at risk, a high-stakes crap shoot.

Now the distant roll of surf
The light breeze off the ocean
And the gentle bending of the sea oats
Calls attention to the warming dunes.

EQUINOX

Beijing did not celebrate the equinox
Except for sprays of flowering peach, forsythia,
Lilacs, and a few intrepid daffodils.
The early morning's gimlet rays of Tutankhamen
    gold
That penetrated drapes of atmospheric dust
Was just one more spectacular beginning.

Oldsters in the park across the street performed
    their
Prehistoric tai chi rites in silent unison;
The neighboring construction sites were oddly
    still;
Pigeons on a complicated circuit wheeled and
    tumbled
In the interval between the buildings and the sky.

Westminster Bridge itself vouchsafed no better
    proof
That splendid calm attends a mighty city in
    repose.
But more arresting still was knowing that beneath
    the
Tranquil cloak of slanting sun a potent multitude
    was stirring.

Bamboo only flowers every hundred years,
But when it does, sweet Jesus.

FELLOW TRAVELERS

Y2K has given up the ghost without a fight,
Christ, without a trace, except for scattered
    snickers,
Its name its only lasting legacy,
No clue as to its final resting place.

And where are the perpetrators of this bang-less
    whimper?
Do their CVs tout their roles? Are they profiled in
Who's Who?
Yes, they've submerged, but look here:
Do they hold a grudge?

For several years these Jeremiahs preached of
Power outages, planes spinning to the ground,
Phone relays on the fritz, banking meltdowns,
Whole accounting systems crashing in a pile of
    numbers.

Every institution had its Y2K Compliance Guru
Wielding dictatorial power behind a veil of
    mystery.
But when precisely nothing happened on the date,
    they vanished.
Dark rumors circulate.

Of all the theories, two stand out. One is they've been given
New identities and hunker down in unsuspecting places,
Working for the super-secret Global Cybernetics Institute
Believed to be connected to Bill Gates.

The second and more credible is they're still in place,
But all the rest of us, in thrall to some mysterious force, have come
To disassociate their names and faces from the Y2K affair,
We've simply blanked them out like faces in a Stalin era photo.

But either way, their paths are surely crossing yours,
Perhaps your seatmate on a plane is one,
The motorcyclist waiting at the light,
The man who meets your daughter in a karaoke bar.

The fear is they're concocting a catastrophe so nasty
That your sneers at Y2K will be forever wiped away.
Some say they plan to place an upper limit on the use of vowels,
Others, willing to believe the worst, say consonants.

Preliminary risk assessment research is alarming.
Consider if they just succeed in limiting the use of B's.
Hit the limit, say goodbye to Bible, billabong, and bubble.
How would the third base coach signal the batter to bunt?

HANGZHOU

In Hangzhou repeating themes and concentricity
Inform the landscape, nothing left to chance.
Its famous lake contains a manmade island
That itself shows off a tiny lake.

A peddler with a toy bamboo whistle
Contrives a piercing birdcall that,
No sooner has its echo died away,
Is picked up in the distance by another,
Then another and another, circuiting the island
Until, returning, it begins again.

Enormous goldfish congregate
Beneath the bridges, some with bulging eyes
And gossamer, mesmerizing fins,
Insolently breathing at the surface,
Alert to movement.
Is it their exhaling that concocts the clinging mist
Now softening the lines of distant buildings
And anointing the foliage of exotic plantings?

Everywhere this Chinese paradise
Has been arranged with taste and strictest
        discipline.
But April wields its own authority.
As early blossoms show themselves,
Suspicions are confirmed that relict species lurk
In crevices between the quarried pavers.

THE CONNOISSEUR OF CHEEKBONES

I am a clinger to cheekbones.
I plant my crampon gaze
Upon these promontories
So as to escape the lasers
Lurking in the pools above.

I have bestrode more cheekbones than
There are Alps and Himalayas,
Visages to me are cheekbones,
Cheekbones visages,
I am the connoisseur of cheekbones.

But you'd be wrong to think
That I am ignorant of
All the atmospherics
Boiling off the features
At the fringe of vision.

My outpost exposes everything,
The slightest movement registers
As when a raptor, in pursuit of prey,
Is yet alert to danger
And, descrying rivals, banks away.

I can vault with lightning speed
From craggy cheekbones
Onto foreheads, chins and noses.
But sometimes, truth to say, looking down,
I succumb to vertigo.

No, it's no great distance down,
Snicker if you like,
But mark this if you please,
Even small men throw long shadows
In the light of early morning and at dusk.

ECHOES

The rippling intervals of silence
Cut with whispering,
Tinnitus of the mind, let's say,
Not so much an echo as a faintly ululating
        stillness,
Distant remnant as it were
Of some nonviolent omission
Like background radiation first hypothesized
To solve a cosmic puzzle subsequently verified.

Can this then be the proof of some forgotten
Yet momentous flinch, a hapless hesitation,
An episode of flagging courage
From whence everything descended?
When, then, did I step back from the edge?
Was there a crisis and I blinked and fled?

And when pray did the spikes of passion weaken?
Can the instant now be fixed with certainty when
Youthful bliss in that sweet dawn began to fade,
When vigor palled, no more to
Surge and flow and bring a tingle to the
Fingers, when no more the primal shout of dawn
Swelled in crescendo from the organ of the
        morning sun?

FATHER

Deeply religious men, I think
Are drawn to God instead of drink
Sucked in by His cosmic wink.

Father despised a drink so much he
Oozed contempt for those who'd clutch
A scotch and water as a social crutch.

But he loved to get on his knees and pray,
Did it at the start and the end of day
In an unselfconscious, habitual way.

"Give me a minute to commune in prayer.
I draw strength from the silence there.
Long as I can do it I won't despair."

All this preaching mortified
Me as a teenager deep inside
But at his coffin I cried and cried.

I would pronounce my father dead
Except I still hear what he said.
It ricochets around my head.

SHUCKING THE BAPTIST BACKPACK

I forsook my Southern accent
In an Eastern college when
Its famous Chaplain
Took the Cross
To beat up Southern whites
Enroute to racial equity.
Results were mixed but some,
Himself included,
Counted personal rewards.
Eight centuries ago
The Greeks learned Latin when
Enrico Dandalo of Venice
And a host of Fourth Crusaders
Took the Cross then sacked
Constantinople;
They forewent Jerusalem,
Their loot consoled them.

I forsook my Baptist faith;
I bought the Chaplain's racial politics
But not his moral certainty
That God's our teammate.
Dare one think that secretly he knew
That God is dead, however blessed be his name?
That Christianity, like war,
Is Clausewitz?

The viscous world of age
Disgorges distant memories
Half digested, dripping caustic juices.
I may lack the stamina or stomach
To spelunk these memories again.
The war, the flower children,
Puke on lace, dog shit on patent leather shoes,
Rage and rage,
Deceitful people, hypocrites and plenty
Who descended into Hell with dope and alcohol,
But looming large among the tarnished icons
And the charlatans
The Chaplain bubbles up unmasticated,
Undigested and, sad to say, unshit.

CASTING THE RUNES

He wanted brawny, strapping thoughts, but
I could offer only disembodied words,
Stripped of flesh and muscle,
Gristle and bones exposed,
Words that had long been flayed and pounded;
They would be picked at by the carrion crows
Who leave naught but skeletal detritus.
At least such parts as would survive their
        ravenings
Could be relied on, even if disjointed, to suggest
To him the essence of a brawny, strapping
        thought or two.
If not to him, still, to a few
Who know enough to cast the runes.

TOUR GUIDE

Here's where they fell, he said,
And here, and over here.
Not like Wayne in Sands of Iwo Jima,
No. Not clean, heroic, manly.
Not like that.

Here they fell in pieces
Turned to jelly, hammered, made unrecognizable,
Blown up. Parts vaporized. Parts tossed about
Like shot rock in a mine with no regard
For what belongs to what.
I guess they screamed and whimpered
Long as they could.

And then over there, he said, was where
My great-granddaddy fell.

His whole platoon was brothers,
You know it was like that then.
When the Rebels got done with this white bunch
      here
They lobbed those shells with a vengeance
At the niggers who dared to fight
And those free niggers exploded, balls and all
Just as if they was white.

Some say down in that ravine,
Here he gestured to a low spot in between,
Was parts of both black and white soldiers
Like stew meat in a pot.
And if you looked at the bloody side,
Not the skin side,
You couldn't tell the difference.

He hesitated, sensing that the group was restive,
Then rounded on them, raised his voice and said,
Okay, I'm done, except I'd like to leave you with
    one thought.
Scabs don't form on dead meat.
That your bus waiting in the parking lot?

CHRISTIANS AND LIONS

Nature abhors a balance, always has,
Pitting predators against their prey,
No surprises there.
But when conditions change
Or prey is overhunted, then
The predator's numbers tumble too,
A kind of peristalsis in reverse sets in,
Moving up the food chain, squeezing species
In their turn, creating greater competition
For the dwindling supply of food,
Selecting out the slower or the smaller
Or the toothless or the just plain hapless.
Ask any lion or Christian here to tell the tale.

Your genes survived the Circus Maximus,
Of that we can be certain; we can also say
With full assurance they survived
Encounters on the African savanna and
The meteor that ushered out the dinosaurs.
We can conclude, in short,
Your DNA's well edited,
No other explanation fits the facts.
Will it succeed from here on out?
That depends on how it measures up today
To changed conditions, overhunting,
And of course, on whether
You're a Christian or a lion.

FATHER AT THE MARGIN

The family legend marked him as a hero.
Generous, kind and funny,
A humble Christian, tithing and devout,
A survivor of poverty and hardship
With broad shoulders but no formal education,
He maximized his options with tenacity and
        character.

As a little boy, apparently,
He coveted a pony, which he could draw from
        memory,
Of course, he never had one, way too poor.
The story is, because he had a
Sickly father and an epileptic sister,
He took a job and left school at fifteen.
This fugitive from Dickens,
This boy who never had a pony
Courageously assumed a man's responsibilities.

But I remember most the evenings with my father
In the years my older brother, struggling
        through the
Tides of adolescence, managed to offend him.
He'd grow apoplectic and abusive.
A rising tide of shouts and blows and crashes
Disrespected doors and pillows,
Penetrating self-protective walls,
A shock wave that shattered all before it,
Violating everything that mattered and was holy.

Later it was other things that got him going.
Usually I think it had to do with work.
Unexpectedly a thing would set him off.
He'd hyperventilate and shriek profanity and
    insults,
Then would tear out to the car,
And roar away without his headlights.

We could hear the squealing tires forever,
Then we'd hold our breaths and swallow sobs,
Impaled upon the skewers of his anguish and his
    pain,
Until at last he coasted to the curb in front,
And struggled up the stairs, ashamed and spent.

BEACHES

One encounter in his rakish twenties
With a self-contained and glorious girl
Had caused confusing things to happen
Like unexpected tears provoked
By buskers in a subway tunnel.

Her blue streak conversation
Launched many moving targets.
Slightly terrifying, too,
She could swim for miles and run.
Her streaky hair stood out behind her
In the wind she made
Striding through admiring streets.

He took her to a hidden place he found
With pungent smells and solitude,
The sea was close at hand
And in the dooryard of the ancient saltbox
Flowers bloomed impulsively without assistance.

On the porch, the sunset at their backs,
Surrounded by the sounds the summer twilight
      makes,
Katydids and crickets and the distant call of
      nightjars,
Oh-so distant,
Whippoorwills and once a dog fox sharply
      barking,
Evening thickened into darkness

Like treacle sheeting on a spoon.

They took morning walks on beaches
Where proprietary gulls patrolled the salty wind
        and
Sandpipers motored in and out of danger
Inches from the speeding edge of surf.

Some days the sun would skip across the
        undersides
Of brilliant clouds, and carom off the
Lazy waves which heaved themselves
        percussively upon the shore,
Sprayed rainbows out like fireworks,
Then hissed and effervesced around their feet.

On some stretches preternatural forces
Gathered sand the size of marbles,
Further on the grains would be as fine as dust,
Some puzzling sorting principal at work.

She sometimes wore a threadbare cotton dress
Scandalously short, her long legs straight and
        strong,
And every starfish, every shell, deserved attention
In the mornings on the shingle when they
Strolled together barefoot holding hands.

Once a storm had left a shelf of waist high sand
Stretching like a bowstring up the beach,
Converging in the distance with the line of
        breakers

And the marching dunes picked out by clumps of
 sea oats.
He charmed her into going on ahead
And she, herself the moving target now,
Became the focus of a single point perspective.

VIXEN

Nineteen days into the new year
On a dusting of new snow so thin
It only partially submerged the larger leaves
A big fox made her strawberry blonde entrance
From the woods down into the field
That slopes to our house like an amphitheater.

Her paws almost disdained the ground entirely
As she strutted down in her luxurious fur,
Traversing from side to side for maximum effect,
Posing first in profile, then full face,
Closer and closer until, satisfied, she languorously
    sat,
Curled her tail excessively about her feet, and
    watched
Our two tomcats stage the damnedest ruckus on
    the porch.

BERNICE

Midafternoon, Bernice emerged from her
    apartment,
Turned west into the light breeze of October and
Set out with measured step and fixed expression.

She held her raincoat closed
With the same hand that clasped
The empty Prada bag, while with
The other redirected absently a few
Escapees from the elegant French braid
Perfected years before time's prism had
Revealed the hundred hues and textures hiding
In her heavy chestnut mane of winsome memory.

Distracted as she passed the pet shop window,
She searched the dim interior uncertainly,
Brightened at a pair of mewling puppies,
Said something intimate and indistinct,
Then, straightening, resumed her pace.
Today was shopping day.

Entering Treasure Island,
She claimed a shopping cart.
Going first to produce, she
Stopped doubtfully before the lettuce.
The escarole looked fresh but slightly coarse.
She selected endive and radicchio, then rolled on.
Fresh thyme and artichokes found their way into
    the basket,

Plus a package of late season blueberries.
Mushrooms, her special expertise, came next.
She chose the portobellos and some small porcinis
    from Yunnan.

Gourmet ingredients had their own location,
    grouped by country.
Bernice carefully examined half a dozen extra
    virgin olive oils,
Opting for the brand on sale though, heaven
    knew, no bargain.
A jar of cornichons from Nice occasioned long
    deliberation;
But eventually, with obvious misgivings, she
    went for
Small sweet gherkins cut with pickled onions
And a can of ripe Greek olives with the pits.

Seafood was her special weakness and she
Quickly claimed a can of backfin crabmeat,
Most expensive of the several crabmeat choices;
At the meat display another patron helped her
Wrestle two large legs of lamb into her cart.

Bernice now turned the corner to the checkout,
Took her place in line and waited.
But before her turn had come
An older man approached.
"Hello, Bernice. Nice to see you."
"Why thank you. Have we met?"
"Oh, yes, of course. I'm John, the manager."
"Perhaps I should complain about the prices;

    really, some of these…"
"Forgive me, but you needn't go through that…"
"No, really, why this virgin olive oil…"
"Bernice, may I ask you if you have the means to pay?"
This was delivered quietly; a pensive silence followed.
Then, as if on impulse, Bernice opened the empty Prada bag.
"Why I do believe I left my billfold in my other purse at home.
If you'll just hold these things I'll go retrieve it and return directly."
Turning with great dignity, she left the store clutching her raincoat with
The hand that held her purse. Watching her go, her interlocutor stood quietly
Until she passed from sight; he then commenced restocking the items in her cart.

TIRE IRON

Summer sounds carried in the city
In the sweltering afternoon
They could convulse you
Like a dose of ipecac
Secreted in a drunk's cheap wine.

The garage's open door and clerestory windows
With their sightless, opaque panes,
The baking tongue of concrete that
Projected insolently toward the street,
Pantomimed a lifeless head
A rictus mutely screaming in the desiccating heat.

No movement showed within
But with a sudden flourish
A piercing ring of steel on rock
Skewered the quiescent air,
Unmistakably a tire iron
Thrown violently onto smooth concrete
Deep inside the dark interior.

Hastily it faded but not before its jarring note had
Triggered a quick spasm of the gut,
And tightened shoulder muscles like a cramp,
Penetrating surely to the psyche
Like a bee sting spreads its poison in a toe.

Gnats swam uncertainly through heavy sunlight,
Picking paths among the dust motes
In suspension at the door.

Exaggerated retching,
Then a tall thin man in coveralls and boots,
Wearing a greasy welding hat and
Black oil smears on wizened cheeks
Oblivious to the heat,
An older man, whose posture told a tale,
Expressed himself, his steps uncertain, lurching,
Held himself as if he had dry heaves,
And, blinking at the fullness of the sun,
Sat with deliberate moves upon the scorching
        curb,
Muttered briefly, then, constricting, shouted.

"Frank you malevolent, overbearing bastard,
You schmuck,
You have no soul, you interfere,
You have no sense of privacy, of dignity,
You're meddling in my business, Frank."

Cradling his chin
The man was heard to say more quietly,
"And do I ever miss a day of work?"

The stifling heat reclaimed the afternoon
A pregnant hush, then finally
With misleading overtones of metal on concrete
From somewhere deep inside
Came a bottle slackly rolling

Toward the street. Down the driveway
Came the bottle, gaining, slowing, slewing,
Unmistakably an empty bottle rolling to the street.

Summer sounds carried in the city
In the sweltering afternoon
They could convulse you
Like a dose of ipecac
Secreted in a drunk's cheap wine.

DEATH AND TAXES

Tax day come and gone
And ice still in the ponds, rafts of it,
Dirty and riding low, but still there,
Defying the thin sunshine with such meanness
You'd not know which way to bet
If you hadn't outlived a few cruel Aprils before.

No sign of greening either in these woods.
But as I go I hear a chickadee, and the
Ravings of a big woodpecker,
Something scuffling in the leaves,
And far away, perhaps imagined, singing.
Still woods are never quiet if you're listening.

My eye picks out a tiny crimson eft
Staggering along the muddy track ahead,
Rowing one leg stiffly at a time.
And then, accustomed, I make out another,
Only a few feet separating them,
Yet no sign that either knows about the other
Until I gather both into a cupped hand
For warmth.

They will not live another year,
They've just emerged triumphant from the great
Ordeal of their short lives,
They survived the only winter they will know.
Their squirming in my fist tickles.

I have walked this track with children
Clinging to each index finger.

Some beeches I pass are diseased.
A kind of fungus marks the bark, discolors it.
Before they topple shelves of scalloped growths
        appear.
Full one in ten contracts it every year, a kind of
        tithe.
And what's a tax if not involuntary tithing?
You might well ask, what living thing should be
        allowed
To live out its allotment without feeding other life
Even as it draws its nourishment
From what has gone before, from the rotting duff
That spreads itself untidily upon the forest floor?
Funguses on living trees are witness to this truth:
Life and death are fellow travelers in the woods.

I recall advice I heard millennia ago:
Never warm cold-blooded things since
When you stop, they die.
Chagrined, I stoop and redeposit my companions
Upon the chilly earth beside the track.

Looking up I see a crow preening in a tree ahead.
He lets me near, then when I cross a line
That only he can see
He gives harsh warning
And the white pine he's protecting comes alive,

A hundred members of his clan
Break cover screaming insults.
But these are crows; it's nothing personal.

The sentinel has disappeared
Along with the flock; I never saw him fly.
Where are the children
Who walked with me? I turn
And see only my own footprints.
Some of the beeches here are straight and clean,
What will become of them?
Will they too disappear?

Near the place where I released the efts
I pause, but see that they are gone.
Yet I do not fear for them.
A child once shared with me her absolute
        conviction
That crimson efts can have no natural enemies.

Returning toward the ponds
I seem to hear but disbelieve my ear,
What with the ice still there and all,
Spring peepers in full voice.

MANAGER'S CALL

On the mound he takes the signal,
Toes the rubber, checks the runners,
Drills a fastball through the zone waist high,
An indisputable called strike.

Taking the return he rubs the ball,
Shakes off the first but not the second signal,
Whips a curve a touch outside and low
That tempts the batter and eludes his swing.

With the leeway of an oh-and-two
He fires an inside pitch with lots of heat
But arguably wild, an HBP
But for the batter's pirouette.

Then what had been intended as a slider
Hangs and drops without momentum
Ending in the dirt and evening the count;
He juggles the rosin bag and drops it.

If a pitcher's stuff is seen to weaken,
Bottom of the eighth, a one run lead, with two
    away
And two on base, what's a manager to do?
Convene a conference on the mound.

Will there be a signal to the bullpen,
Or merely words of inspiration?
In eight innings he's allowed three hits
And fanned twelve batters, but he's tired.

This lefty knows that whether his earnest pitch
To see the inning out succeeds or fails,
His bright career could end up in the ditch;
A manager's thumb is always on the scales.

LATE IN THE DAY

Tired from setting up bins and tables
I taped my hand lettered sign on the church door:
Rummage Sale Saturday.
Bring your Rummage Friday.

Sprawling on the bench inside
The little park next to the church
I fumbled in my pocket
For a cigarette that I lit and dragged on.

"You shouldn't do that. It will make you sick."
Spoken by the little girl pushing her sister on the
        swing.
She faced me now and
Speared me with enormous eyes.

Guiltily I took a final hit and
Stubbed it out, then like old men
Will do to ease the tension,
Asked a silly question.

"Who do you think the person was
Who made that sign?" I pointed.
She said, "Maybe Michael.
He's fourteen. He lives with us.

He used to practice signs on
Rolls of wrapping paper that he stole
From his stepfather's butcher shop.
Michael usually sleeps all day.

He paints signs at night. On buildings."
More discomfort, so I changed the subject.
"Where's your mother?" "Working."
"So you're caring for your sister?"

"She's not my sister. She's my friend.
She needs an operation on her lip."
I had to veer away again.
"Where do you live?"

She pointed to the shrubs beside the church
That shielded several cardboard boxes.
Shocked, I asked, "What do you eat?"
"Whatever Jesus sends us."

Late in the day I came back to the park
I had a bag of burgers and some milk.
The little girls were gone.
The empty boxes and the swing were there, but
        still.

SELF HELP

As if preferring only one direction
Like a mountain stream,
Or pinballs headed south despite all intervention,
Happiness descends progressively to apathy,
Ennui, anxiety, and deep despair,
As surely as warm bodies cool.

The trick's to find some outside source
Of energy to ratchet up again —
A downpour gets the freshet flowing fresh,
A nickel used to keep the pinballs coming,
And a brawny guy can always push the boulder
        up the hill.

Outside support is justifiable,
Even simple souls protect themselves.
Derelicts take shelter in the rain,
Neanderthals invented herbal remedies for pain.
Your path to health may be in advertising,
"Attractive boulder seeking Sisyphus."

LEFT HANGING

Left hanging. Infirmities proliferate.
Waiting, *sine die*. Excessive leisure.
End game drags uncertainly.
Eating, sleeping, desultory conversation.
Thoughts that concentrate the mind.

Back then before you even knew
How tall you'd grow, an optimistic leap
Could always get you to the lowest limb,
But bravery in short supply,
You'd save the serious climbing for tomorrow.

Back in the day I recognized as lies
The claims that smoking was benign.
I helped emasculate the facts.
I'd say, "This one won't kill me,"
Forty times a day or more.

I broke the fever finally
In time to save my firstborn
All that secondary smoke.
This, while hardly serious climbing
Is enough. Will have to be.

OUT BACK

Early one June morning out back
Where the grass is neglected,
Way out past the gate where
People almost never go,
I saw a man with a shovel
Bury something big, then
Put back the grass clods
And stomp them down with his heel.

It wasn't so far away that I
Couldn't make out his old dog
Looking left and right and
Fidgeting like he expected trouble
But I guess none came
Since soon enough the man
Gathered up a big piece of
What looked like burlap
And the shovel and threw them
In the back of his truck.

The old dog needed help jumping up
To the bed of the truck that
The man didn't give him,
And when the man drove over to the
Dirt road and disappeared
The old dog just sat there looking.

MEN'S EUROPEAN FIGURE SKATING CHAMPIONSHIPS 1994

Where do they get it, these young men?
Where do they mine the spit and grit to spend
    those years
Those terrifying years
In cloistered competition
With themselves?

What's the prize to mesmerize and focus them?
What's the force that drives them and their peers
Those super-athlete peers
To superhuman feats on ice?

When do they first suspect the lie?
When do they appreciate that championship
springs only from
Those triple axel jumps?

Who's next upon the ice?
Whose neck upon the ice is bared to fall or
hesitation?

How to choose from such perfection? The winner
    is

WHERE HAVE YOU GONE, JOE DIMAGGIO?

If life were but a property of matter
And reason a configuration of the mind,
And elation and depression the seesaw ends
Of serotonin out of balance in the brain,
If dreams were merely side effects of neural
Recharge during sleep,
Then Tenzing, Hillary and Mallory,
Those incoherent avatars,
Would make more sense.

In thrall to their compulsions,
Gripped by their genetic programs,
One might say that
Two were destined to succeed and one to fail
As they were inescapably themselves
And it was there.

Could Hemingway have given up before he did?
He'd lost it, certainly he knew it,
Yet he struggled on for years.
Was his miasmic downward spiral
DNA's geometry writ large?
Were the very bar stools on Bimini foretold,
Along with that transfixing paragraph
That started his farewell to arms?
He surely meant his suicide as proof
That he was capable of action in the end,
And yet, and yet.

Could Joe Dimaggio have petered out unsung
In some backwater double A charade?
Or was his grace and dignity, his spare precision,
His balletic poise an ineluctable result of
        chemistry?

In 1941 the Yankee Clipper sired a little man.
Young Joe grew up resembling his father,
Went off to Yale from prep school,
Strong and capable to all appearances,
Handsomer, more polished than his dad,
But struggling to escape his father's shadow,
Did not extend himself and those who'd met him
Hardly missed him when he dropped out
        sophomore year.
He never talked about the man whose name he
        bore
But once, drinking, he confided that his stepmom
Had called him on the phone before she died,
She'd told him what she'd done,
He'd been the last to hear her famous voice alive,
But no he hadn't tried to help,
He lived too far away.

In 1999 a small report in *Time* disclosed his death.
Even here he was occluded
By his father, whose death provoked great fits of
National mourning only months before.
Joe Junior, 57, reclusive and penurious,
His father's only son,

A sometime junkyard worker, had passed away
Somewhere in California, presumably
Of natural causes.

THE ACTOR

In my dream about a play
An actor, in a turgid scene,
Is seen to drop a line,
Then grimaces, gesticulates
As if in pain, slumps to the floor
And dies, convincingly, before your eyes.

But did he die because he'd dropped the line,
Or did he drop the line because he was about to die?
On this depends the whole interpretation of the play.
In working through the paradox, you may well ask,
"So did the actor really die? You said it was a play."
I said it was a dream.

NAMES

A Buryat friend, a poet, comes tonight.
He sings of the Oka and Geser,
And of delicate relations
Among trees and brooks and grasses.
He'll work his way along the rocky path
That traverses our dooryard.
He'll likely see the rings of tiny pastel flowers
That surround each large protruding rock.

These little flowers are as common
Here in May as bird songs
And are known to every native
Like a folk song or tradition
Yet they seem to have no name.

Perhaps he'll see in them
Suggestions of Buryatia which
Just now is nearly ready to erupt with blooms.
Perhaps they'll sing a bit to him.
Perhaps they'll stir his poet's need
To quicken visual impressions
And verify the actuality of living things
By naming them.
Perhaps he'll ask, "What are they called?"

Some years ago when we were touring Sichuan,
Schlepping our unaccustomed frames up
      mountains
We'd seen Chinese paintings of but disbelieved

Until we'd climbed the treacherous trails and
Leapt the cataracts,
We'd taken breathless notice of a largish bird
Of royal blue, its graceful, rakish tail
Flicking in disdainful disregard
Of rhododendron in precarious places
And all the elevated sweetness that our guide
Whose name was Zhou Xiaoping
Called his back yard.

We'd asked Zhou what its name was.
He'd hesitated overlong,
But then in perfect English said
It was a Sichuan long-tailed blue bird,
After which we'd shared conspiratorial smiles.

THIRTIETH COLLEGE REUNION

The carnival began with men on stilts,
Juggling their old routines,
Studiously ignoring tightrope acts
Being performed by famous colleagues
In the spotlight high above them.
This gave way to dogs and ponies,
Trained seals and dancing bears,
Breathless performers sprinting
Around the ring of recollection,
Nostalgia balanced on the back of bathos.

Then the clowns arrived, as if
They'd sprung from some dyspeptic dream.
With bellies, flashing yellow teeth and neon
    noses,
Trading pratfalls for attention,
Full of bonhomie, they
Slapped each other's rounded backs and
    guffawed.

Jerky squints gave way to measured glances
In the search for youthful faces lurking
In the etchings and the dewlaps and the jowls,
Long unspoken names appeared from nowhere
Just in time to do the introductions
With surprise that was disguised by smiling eyes.

Someone had the idea to recite the
Names of classmates who had died.
They browsed the interval from Tet to AIDS,
And dwelled on strokes and suicide.
The hallway marble was inscribed
With seven classmates' names.
Others who'd escaped the war
To concentrate on equities and fame
Had nonetheless been taken by the throat
And exited with nothing more to show
Than a brace of kids in prep school,
Modest debts, a house in Greenwich,
And a paid-for *New York Times* obit.

Then there were those whose dignified
Defeats by fearful ailments known by Latin
    names
Had raised the bar of courage, yet
Had left us somehow thinking
That we owed them and we failed them
At the end.

But one had died obscurely
With no glory and no shrine,
His miasmic death an understated
Counterpoint to those ecstatic days of youth
When alabaster clouds sailed through the
Oceans of the sky
And it seemed that just by willing,
He could fly.

Nothing in his final days
Recalled his early promise
Or gave witness to his wit.
Nothing, that is, but the quaint announcement
That he'd scratched on soiled paper
And had mailed a week before his death
With no return address:
Emmett Kelly sends regrets.

FIFTIETH HIGH SCHOOL REUNION

When I heard the reunion was set
For October I thought with regret
That I'd have to miss it
Because of explicit
Intentions to be in Tibet.

But pneumonia and heart complications
Circumvented Chinese aspirations
Since the air in Beijing,
Xi'an and Chongqing
Undermines and negates medications.

The smog leaves you hoarse and demeaned.
You feel like your clock has been cleaned.
With weak lungs and ticker
I was loath to get sicker
And was glad when my doc intervened.

He said, "Can this ridiculous plan!
You're not indestructible, man!
Your lungs will become
Anaerobic, you bum!
Bail out of the trip if you can!"

So I leapt from my hospital bed
Looking old and a bit underfed.
And with my trophy wife,
The joy of my life,
I bailed out and came here instead.

I don't mind acknowledging, though,
That I was concerned I would blow
Recognizing my peers
After all of these years
So I practiced just saying, "Hello."

It turns out my fears were undue
The name tags are helpful, it's true,
And we've all preserved traces
Of our teenager faces
But here's my point of view.

Old age, it turns out, is a bitch
Unlike high school with nary a glitch
When the only concerns
Were excessive sunburns
Term papers and zits and jock itch.

We're losing our hearing, and shoot,
Our eyesight is failing to boot.
Our parts are synthetic
Or outright prosthetic
And the flatulence problem's acute.

We teeter and stumble and sway
What hair that's remaining is gray.
With our wrinkles and jowls
And explosive bowels
We're nobody's jonquil bouquet.

But jeez, the alternative's worse.
Old age is a damnable curse,
Yet it's hardly absurd
That it's greatly preferred
To that ride in a Cadillac hearse.

The moral I hope to evoke
Is as modern as it is baroque
You play out your hand
Looking eager and tanned
Cause it's over the minute you croak.

HOLY LAND UPDATE

Bulldozers raze some homes in Gaza, driving one
Evicted son to blow himself and Haifa revelers to
    smithereens,
Whereupon a cousin of a Haifa diner opens fire
    on Arabs in a mosque,
Then one who dodged his bullets blows a theatre
    in Netanyah, killing six.

Choppers shoot that miscreant with rockets in his
    car, taking with him
Several incidental passers-by whose orphaned
    boys are energized
To sneak a bomb onto a bus somewhere in Tel
Aviv that kills a dozen;
Their deaths provoke more housing demolitions in
    the Gaza camps.

Why should the keening widows in Ramallah and
    Jerusalem
And their respective menfolk doubt the wisdom of
    this ancient feud?
This is the way it is, and was, and ever shall be,
World without end, amen, amen.

GOP EMPATHY, TO BE CONTINUED

I've never known politics meaner;
The GOP's standard demeanor
Is to cheer execution,
The standard solution
For any alleged misdemeanor.

"The defendant's attorney was snoozing?
He showed up in court after boozing?
Disregard dereliction —
Uphold the conviction!"
Moral certainty practically oozing.

And what of the uninsured bloke
Who is comatose after a stroke?
"Medication must halt,
It's his own blooming fault."
Compassion? A cruelty joke.

TO MY CHINESE COLLEAGUES

We found one voice for two great cultures
And declared environment to be one common
        heritage,
Our shared responsibility.
In doing so we forged enduring friendship
That assures our paths will cross again.

SMOKING IN A BEIJING TAXI

Beijing's a dubious place to foster recollections
Of Virginia growing up, but today a taxi driver
Lights a cigarette in traffic on the Third Ring
      Road,
And though he cups his hand outside the car,
A vagrant tendril finds my nose and
Sends me on a trip no madeleine could muster.

That tiny whiff of smoke, an indistinct suggestion,
Blasts the neat arrangement of my thoughts,
And conjures visions long since buried with the
      image of
Tobacco as a smart, appealing, status-reaffirming,
Sex-enhancing, perfect adjunct to the perfect life.

My smoking days were filled with teenage girls in
      cars
With glowing skin and limpid mocking eyes,
As sure of their unfolding beauty and appeal
As any butterfly, and as elusive to the touch.
They'd deign to let me light their Herbert
      Tareytons,
Steadying my hand with theirs,
Perhaps they'd tease my elbow with a squeeze,
And sometimes even tolerate a kiss
Before they disappeared, abandoning their smokes
To smolder in the dashboard ashtray.

To gripe about a girl who smoked was common
      with some guys.
For me, tobacco on their breaths spelled female
      sexuality.
It laid bare the diffident brown wren
As self-assured seductress, co-conspirator,
It transformed her very breathing into
      provocation.

And one, with glistening sable hair, whose cruelty
Outdid her stunning looks, could flick her ashes
      out the window
And dismiss me with complete finality. For those
      who
Held her interest, she contrived humiliating
      competitions
That she monitored implacably with drags upon
      her Chesterfield.
Her special chum, remote and chiseled, said to be
      a family friend,
Though they were rumored to be lovers,
Would lend her his green Oldsmobile convertible,
Which she would drive alone, top down, hair
      streaming.

But now, intruding crazily, absurd and yet
      transporting,
Is the recollected odor of the car I owned in high
      school,
A beguiling mix of flocked upholstery, rubber
      floor mats,
Leather baseball gloves, stale beer, old socks and

        chewing gum,
And lingering suggestions of tobacco and
        perfume.

That glorious Ford, that old Swiss Army knife of
        cars,
Was sanctuary, refuge, office, restaurant,
confessional and flophouse.
At the barbecue waitresses on skates brought
Trays of food that balanced in the window
        apertures,
At drive-in movies speaker boxes did the same,
And in the trunk there rode an odd assortment of
        provisions
Just in case: a bathing suit, a football, an old
        blanket,
And sometimes, depending on the bank account, a
        spare.

The voices of companions and the honking traffic
Mingling with the radio just then inventing rock
        and roll,
And the slurping downdraft carburetor and
        exhaust note
Of the flat-head V-eight engine as we cycled
        through the gears
Crescendoed and diminished endlessly, for we
        were young.

Today the taxis clog the Third Ring Road
And slow the pace of traffic.

MOTHER'S FUNERAL

At long last, dear, I lowered you
Into the ground where your darling has slept
These thirty years and more,
I might have thrown in token dirt
Except the dirt was hidden
Under poignant yards of tasteful astro turf
Which also blocked the fetching smell of earth,
A smell I craved the way a farmer
Craves the loamy smells of April
When the soil is ready to receive the seed
And burial means renewal.

Turning from that hole, taken more by
What I did not feel than what I felt,
Braced for searing grief, or anguish,
Even guilty thoughts, but finding none,
I wondered what cosmetic shield
Protected, sealed me from sensation,
Covered the pungent stuff in which
Relationships are buried, those
Cadavers of old loves reduced by age,
Forgetfulness and yes, ennui, interred
Before the flesh is cold,
Sealed in a time capsule against the
Chance that in the end she might be right
About eternal life.

My numbness should have come as no surprise.
I'd said goodbye to her a dozen times
Before her sight had gone,
Before she'd fallen, fracturing her hip,
Before her hip was pinned,
Before the bedrails and the wheelchair,
Before the lights behind her eyes had dimmed.
I trapped her sweetness in my
Private amber long ago,
And now I'd turned away unmoved
From her diminished corpse.

She'd prayed for death for years
During her lucid intervals,
Which tapered off
Like dripping from a leaking reservoir
That empties over time.
Was her death some kind of
Providential grant? And if so
Why so slow in coming,
Why delayed until the lucid moments ceased,
The horrid illnesses,
The accidents,
Infirmities of age,
The soiled diapers,
Incoherence,
Why not better timing, then?
Still, an answer is an answer.
Maybe, though, the trick's in what you ask for;
Pray for death and soon enough,
You'll get results; just don't pray for earthly
Immortality.

Clearly, dear, I've thinking yet to do.
Perhaps you will be privy to
My thoughts and queries on these things.
I doubt it, but Pascal convinced me of the
Foolishness of jumping to conclusions.
On the chance, then, dear old girl,
Here's to you.

MABEL AND MARGARET

Mabel, as an infant, had been named for his dear
    mother,
Margaret, named for nobody, was Mabel's
    younger brother.
There is not a speck of truth to rumors they were
    queer,
Margaret was a barrister, and Mabes an engineer.

One thing that distinguished them was Mabes'
    confusing handle,
It stuck to Mabes eternally, like dogshit to your
    sandal.
Margaret who, it must be told, acquired no catchy
    label,
Out of spite and meanness always called his
    brother Mabel.

Prodigious in geometry, with abstract thought at
    ease,
Our Mabes saw life from every angle — radians
    and degrees.
Trumped in math and science, Margaret honed
    linguistic arts;
In blaspheming and swearing he became a man of
    parts.

If our two heroes separate paths to happiness
    ascended,
Yet both loved singing all the songs their father
    recommended.
And both could waterski and shoot and change a
    throw-out bearing,
Which often stimulated wondrous looks and
    jealous staring.

Each of them was prone to slightly moralistic
    preaching,
And sometimes stooped to revel in didactic
    overreaching.
But mostly with each other they were meek and
    unassuming,
Except when Mabes attacked attorneys, vicious,
    dark and fuming.

To these forays our Margaret would respond with
    quiet pride
That rants ne'er take the citadel where lofty
    thoughts reside.
That evenness and reason are the qualities to
    treasure,
Let loose such fulminations, you'll repent them at
    your leisure.

Occasionally Margaret himself would scream and shout
On some crusade respecting which he entertained no doubt.
Mabes would blame the problem on those cultural destroyers,
Those paradigms of evil and chicanery, the lawyers.

The truth is they were pretty much two peas in a Pequod
Like Ishmael and Queequeg when you pierce the thin façade.
Now they're old and feeble, and occasionally dwell
On modest exploits years ago, their sins, and fears of Hell.

THE PRIZED IF UNFORESEEN REWARD

The pillbox filled on Sundays
Once again has emptied out.
Another week has trickled through my fingers.
How the diminishing supply
Bids up the price of weeks!

More precious now than when in youth
The glistening future stretched ahead
Eternal and unknowable.
It was nothing to squander a week then
In desultory dreams and reading.

Unknowable? Well, that was then.
Now known, at least the parts
Remembered, and the rest forgotten,
And presumed, if not remembered,
Unimportant and forgettable,
But I repeat myself.

As manhood drips away,
Nostalgia mixes weirdly with relief,
There'll be no more excruciating tests
Of strength, agility, or brilliance.

Competitors become companions
As the weeks progress, with
Laughter and tranquility,
The prized if unforeseen reward
For merely lasting up to now.

ANCIENT AND ABRADED HILLS

Older than the ancient and abraded hills, I am yet
Fresher than the mountain streams that ground
       them
From their awful, primal splendor into
Landscapes tame enough to pet and plunder.

Now the Chinese children run and shout
Beneath their parents' darting eyes, and neither
       the
Wizened men on benches nor their tiny birds in
       cages
Voice outrage at arrested flight.

Once all coiled springs and portent I remain
Inchoate like a volunteer tomato vine
Whose blossoms in the late September sun
Will be remembered, but as gestures, not as fruit.

"Wanbao, wanbao." Hawking papers from a
       platform bike
A white-haired man with tiny eyes quite far apart
Appears each evening and then disappears,
From whence to whence great Oriental mysteries.

SIXTY

Chinese bike mechanic does his business on the sidewalk
Tools and parts bestride his three-wheel flatbed cargo bike.

Cargo bikes abound, no two alike,
The Chinese urban beast of burden,
Used for moving everything from fridges to live pigs,
Also good for sleeping in the shade,
Transporting Grandma to the dentist,
And excursions almost anywhere with colleagues
Hunkered on the platform, arguing and smoking.

Practiced in their art as any athlete,
Cargo bikers radiate proficiency,
But focus on the traffic, rarely speak.
They squint against the sun
And disregard pedestrians and two wheel bikes,
But yield to four or six wheel entities,
Confucian to the core.

These soap and water virgins can be
Cautious drivers mindful of the head of steam
That builds behind a moving load of bricks or garbage
Or outrageous gamblers with the complex laws of motion
That inform the streaming flow of vehicles.

But unlike manic taxi drivers with their frenzied
> honking,
Cargo bikers are the Stoics of the road, impassive.

They maintain their own contraptions, never
> seeking help
From any sidewalk bike mechanic, even though in
> transit
To and from his square of sidewalk he's a
> member of their guild.
Though their ages range from twelve to god
> knows what,
The grizzled ones keep pace with ease and grace,
And when they ride in gangs they own the street.
One is moved to think that sixty doesn't have to
> be a bitch.

THE ANARCHY OF A ONCE WELL-DISCIPLINED ANATOMY

With unresponsive muscles barely
Clinging to the bones and sinews
That they once controlled so proudly,
Every joint now registers objection
Should their supervisor undertake
A rapid movement or a staircase.
Shit.
Shit? Don't you wish.

UNWELCOME AUTUMN

Lazy leaves loop down in
Sunday morning's chilly sunshine
Their September portent unmistakable.
It's coming now, the brisk
And colorful fruition of another year
Somehow unwelcome and distracting
As the languid summer dissipates
And darkness gains a foothold.

The church bells ending as I near,
A deacon holds the door ajar
And as I pass he looks askance,
But when I shake my head he nods.
The heavy door swings closed.
No comfort there.
Nor in the shadow of these
Impertinently shedding trees.

My saunter past the church
Has jostled old Septembers
Into memory, but confusingly,
The characters that populate those
Apple-crisp and gaudy landscapes
Appear in monochrome,
As dated as daguerreotypes,
Drab, unlike this morning's looping leaves.

No herculean challenge or
Life-threatening test of strength or will
Is forecast yet I somehow cannot
Squelch a vague uneasy fear.

Some grim ordeal may yet
Arrive unheralded
Before the winter solstice,
Explaining why this autumn is unwelcome.

DARKNESS

Waking, struggling through the darkness
Switching off the whining brave new clock
Treading explosively on
Plastic
Pillow
Packaging,
Might as well be drive-by gunshots
Brings my fading dream to a staccato finish.

Managing the hall by feel
As in ten thousand other trips
Some well-lit yet now by feel
Deep morning's ritual needs no light
No more than when relaxing into night.

Counting numbly, blindly, every stair
Now fumbling with the switch that floods the
    kitchen
Not with light but with the reaffirming smell of
Coffee, in which slumber's cobwebs blackly
    vanish.

Seducing me, the promise of another day
Plays out reflectively upon the sky
Shrugged shapes appear to discipline themselves
    outside

Like the older sergeant major who can
Hike his girth up to his shoulders on parade;
He knows he soon will pass the last reviewing
    stand.

POSTSCRIPT

Over the years my writing of poetry, or doggerel, or blank verse, or whatever you choose to call it, has been enabled by family members, about the only people who've read it or had me read it to them. I've tried out various iterations of some pieces to Melissa so frequently that she surely must have thought, "God, not that one again." But her encouragement that I keep writing has never wavered, which I can also say of my daughter Victoria, a high school English teacher, my sister Jean, her husband Jim, and sons George and Charlie.

This booklet is a maiden effort of sorts. Though my sporadic verse writing has extended over decades, the lurking hypothesis that more people write poetry than read it has regularly squelched any urge to publish it. I did manage to incorporate some of my pieces into a memoir, *Everything Has a Life (2012),* that I've also included in this collection. But I always figured that if I was the only real audience for my stuff, a standalone book of poems would be a foolish exercise. So what changed?

First, son George (another family poet), suggested that insisting I wrote only for myself was nonsense. Reacting to the only poetry reading I ever participated in, he charged me with *actually taking pleasure* in reading my pieces to others, and, surprised, I had to admit that he was right. Second, my sister Jean (a librarian) and her husband Jim (an English professor and himself a poet, now sadly deceased) have been quite insistent that I should publish. Third, and probably most important, there's that thing about time's wingéd chariot.

I'm deeply grateful to Essex Editions for bringing this booklet to fruition; to George, my daughter Victoria, and my wife Melissa for their wise editorial suggestions; and to the capable and indefatigable Katie Shepard for pulling it all together. This selection of poems and doggerel is a subset of a larger grouping of scribbles. If you think these are weird, you should see the ones I held back.

Gordon Davis
Evanston, IL
December 7, 2018

www.ingramcontent.com/pod-product-compliance
Lightning Source LLC
Chambersburg PA
CBHW070437010526
44118CB00014B/2086